Introduction

MW00616322

If you've ever had a relationship that lasted more than a few minutes, you understand the seismic role lying can play. And if you've ever been in a relationship with a typical male, you understand that a well-timed lie saves hours of wasted time that could have been better spent drinking coffee or enjoying a manicure.

Man is a deceptively complex creature: capable of recalling exact batting averages from twenty years ago yet constantly forgetting to replace the toilet paper roll; fascinated by universal remotes yet completely ambivalent about his daughter's first Halloween costume; able to differentiate between sockets with an eighth of an inch difference yet entirely oblivious to the fact his wife's chopped off three inches of her hair. Women might characterize these deeply embedded traits as selfish—and they'd be exactly right. So how then is a man's significant other supposed to cope with such egregious flaws and maintain sanity?

By lying.

Because the only thing more tragic (and hard to live with) than a man is a man with a bruised ego. Consider this the first-ever couples therapy book that tells it like it is: He's a sometimes loveable idiot who will never change, so try to have some fun with it or you'll lose your freaking mind. These seventy-five white lies are merely a start; an introduction into the satisfying world of fabrication that will—if used liberally—strengthen your relationship.

You're welcome.

I know—watching
sports can be **tiring.**

Are you still a good dancer?!? **What a silly question!**

Didn't you see how I was looking at you from that **dark corner by the bar** while you were out there doing the Running Man?

No one makes a bed like you.

Including **blind** people.

I know. It's **hard to remember** my favorite kind of flower.

Especially when it's an obscure one like lily . . . which also happens to be my name.

Yes. You **absolutely** need $180 state-of-the-art running shoes.

Barbecuing is **totally** high impact.

You're **such** a loyal fan.

It must mean **a lot** to the team that you arrive **an hour** before the players.

You're right—**someone** must have taken your keys.

Maybe it was the **same person** who ordered all that pay-per-view porn.

I think it's **so thoughtful** you leave your toenail clippings scattered around the house for me to find.

They're **little reminders of our love.**

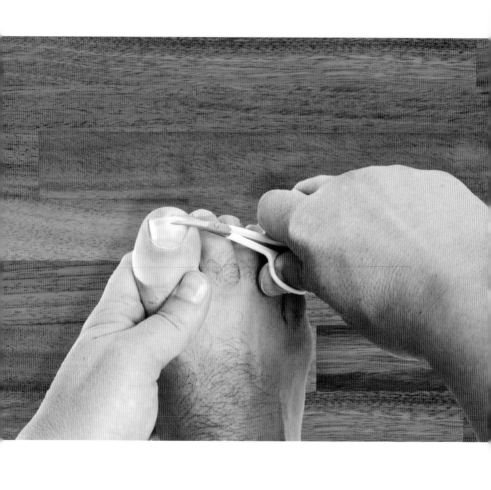

You sure spend **a lot** of time on the Internet once I go to bed.

Sports must **really** pick up after dark.

Choosing the **Final Four over Disneyland** for our family vacation was a great idea.

The kids really appreciate **a good pick and roll** more than they would Space Mountain.

Those sunglasses make you look **just** like Maverick.

Nobody has a sweet Hi-Fi setup like you.

Even if it **hasn't worked since college**, it's still totally boss.

You don't have to tell me **every time** you use the last of the milk or the toilet paper.

I **usually** figure it out when I'm eating dry cereal or sitting on the toilet.

Surprised? **Of course!**

When you said you had a special day planned for us, I **never** would have pictured us at the track.

You're as **charmingly romantic** as you are **financially responsible**.

You guys are just like Clooney's gang in *Ocean's Eleven*. But with farmer's tans.

Thank you for taking care of the plants while I was away.

I should have told you that they need water to live. **My bad.**

I guess we **could** get a Michael Jordan poster for the baby's room.

I was thinking maybe the alphabet, but you're right, **the alphabet didn't win six championships**.

I **love** watching you eat.

It reminds me of our lovemaking: **fast**, **sloppy**, and **reeking of barbecue**.

Too much lighter fluid?
No such thing.

I **love** that tangy chemical taste!

Not many guys still play **Wiffle Ball** in their 40s.

And none that I know keep such detailed statistics. You've **really** got something special going here.

I **love** it when you talk like Yoda.

"Hmmm, blue balls you have, do you?"

"He's more machine now than man, twisted and evil."

It's OK that you threw your plate after that interception. **Really.**

It shows our kids that Daddy's a **man of action.**

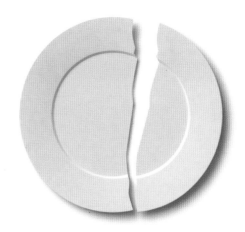

Are you kidding me?
Women **love** hairy backs.

It's like having sex with a
shag rug.

You are the **best karaoke singer** in this place. Easily.

No one has the same drive and determination. It's like they're just doing it for fun.

Honestly, since you shaved your head, I **can't even tell** you're going bald.

It just looks like you've **joined a cult**, that's all.

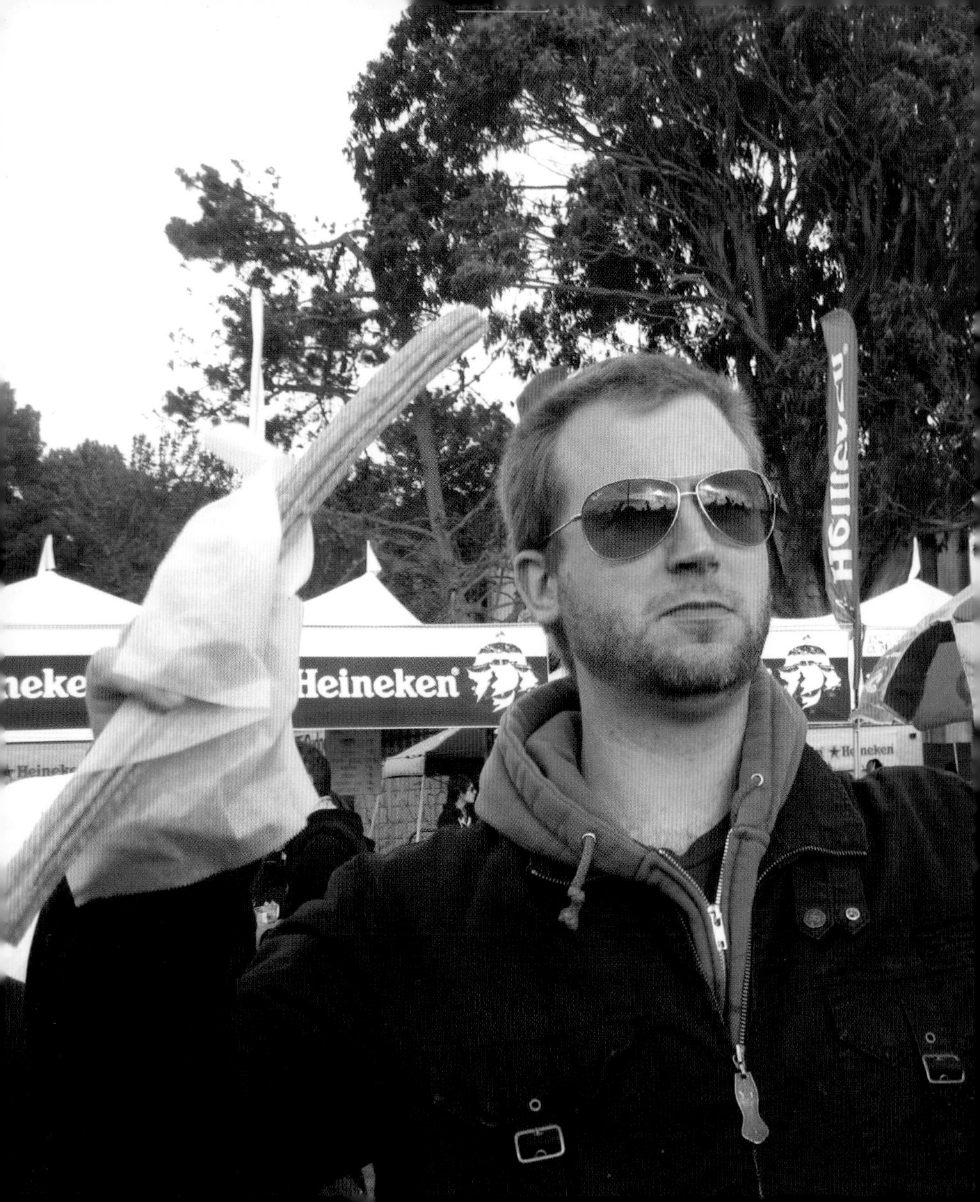
Heineken
Heineken

You're right. It's fine to scarf down fried food **all day.**

I **enjoy** waking up in the middle of the night to you complaining about your tummy ache.

Those scented candles in the bathroom are **purely decorative.**

It's not like you ever need to **light** one, silly.

I **love** your sense of humor!

Putting crap on your head in public **never gets old.**

I can only imagine how **physically draining** hunting must be.

Last I checked, **triggers don't pull themselves.**

It's **so daring** the way you drive on empty.

Getting gas is for **wusses** and **girls**.

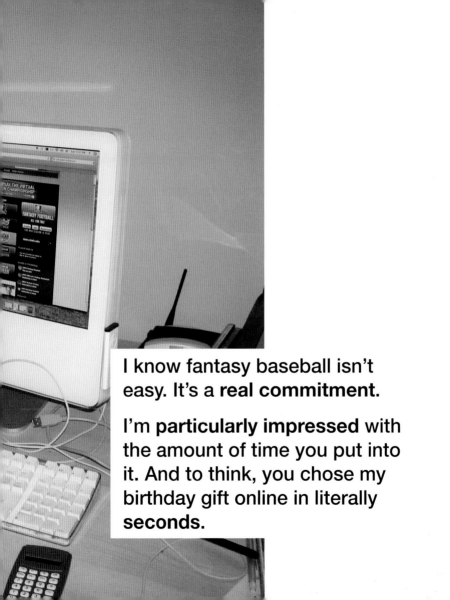

I know fantasy baseball isn't easy. It's a **real commitment**.

I'm **particularly impressed** with the amount of time you put into it. And to think, you chose my birthday gift online in literally **seconds**.

I **love** your spaghetti.

It's **so crunchy!**

You're **definitely** captain of this ship.

Even if it **is** a rental . . . that you don't know how to drive.

Yeah, let's get a pickup!

We can drive around, throw back some Busch, and pick up scrap metal!

I think it's **really mature** that you don't **need** to go out all the time.

You're content just to kick back on a Friday night, watch a movie, and polish off a case. **Good for you.**

It takes a **special type of guy** to pull off the socks and sandals look.

The kind that has never seen a mirror.

You're right. That magician was **totally** lame. You definitely would have been the **better entertainment choice** at our kid's birthday.

Especially if you did that one awesome trick with your eyelid. **Everyone loves that.**

I love watching you play toy versions of instruments you **never learned to play.**

It makes me **so proud.**

It's OK, **a lot** of guys don't know which side of the plate the fork goes on.

But not too many would actually lay it **across** the plate.

Your work buddies are **hilarious.**

Especially the ones who black out **before 10 P.M.**

I like how you always toss your clothes on the floor, *exactly* **fourteen inches** away from the hamper.

That kind of accuracy should help you hit the toilet bowl **someday.**

You look **so sexy** when you play video games!

It's a **real turn-on** to see you in that kick-ass headset **yelling at twelve-year-olds.**

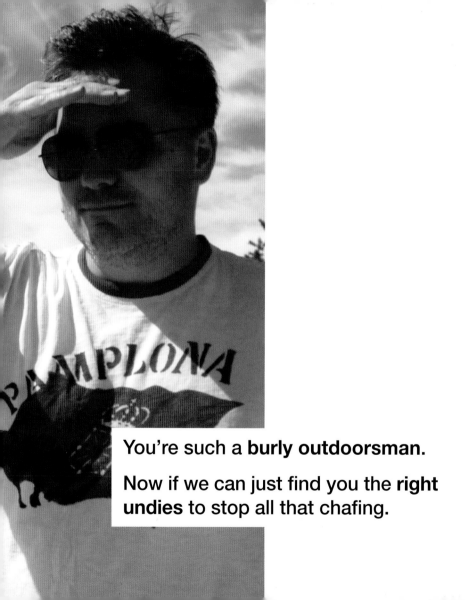

You're such a **burly outdoorsman.**

Now if we can just find you the **right undies** to stop all that chafing.

All our friends love it when you get drunk and talk politics.

Especially when you lay out your **epic** "weed should be free" plan.

So you're rocking the **sport coat and T-shirt** tonight, huh?

Let me give Tubbs a call to see if he wants in.

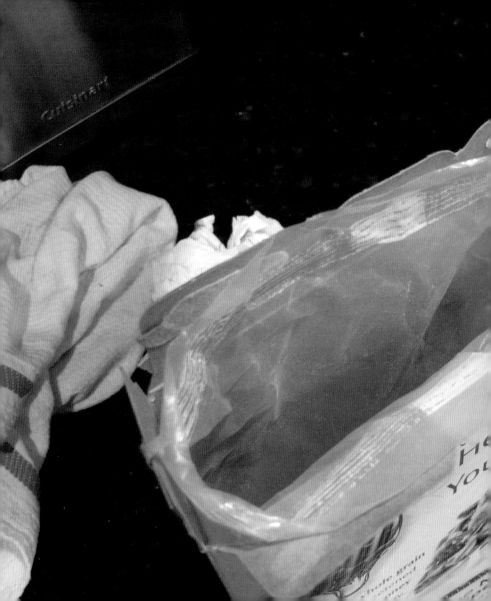

Look for Horizon Organic® Yogurt

...has a full line...

Manage Weight

Go ahead and put that cereal back in the cupboard.

There's no telling how long **four and a half Frosty Os** will last us.

Yes.

Tailgating six hours before the concert was an **awesome** idea.

Your camping trips are **so much fun.**

Who needs groceries and sleeping bags when you have five cases of beer and a VW bus?

I know that foosball is **much, much more than a hobby.**

Even if I don't understand why you need to wear a jersey when you play.

You could still **totally** be
a fireman.

So you're scared of candles—
BFD.

Sure, let's use paper plates again tonight. **You know who eats off paper plates?**

Hillbillies.

And they know how to have a **good time!**

Team jerseys look **so sexy** on you.

I can't tell if you're the handsome, young millionaire pitcher or **the man who struggles to lift the trash.**

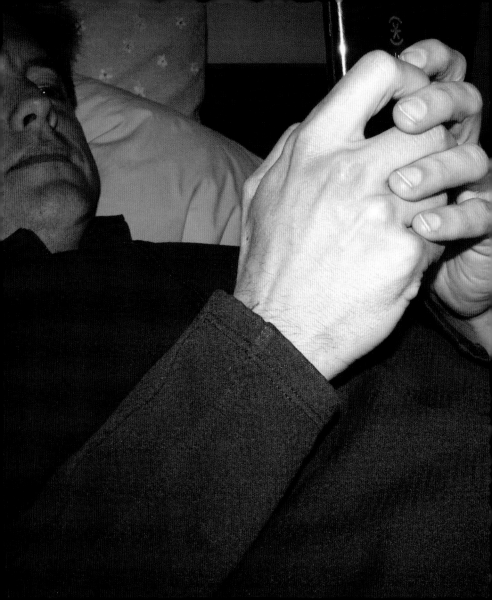

It's **no big deal** that you denied my Friend request.

I know how you **value your privacy** on Facebook.

It's OK that you still like **snacking on Animal Crackers.**

You don't line the animals up in a row anymore or **make elephant noises** and that's a big step forward.

I think that new business plan you guys hatched on the camping trip is a **real winner.**

Who **wouldn't** want their trash taken out by sexy robots?

You're such a **fun** drunk.

Like last Saturday night after the bar when the neighbors caught you peeing on their lawn.

Good times!

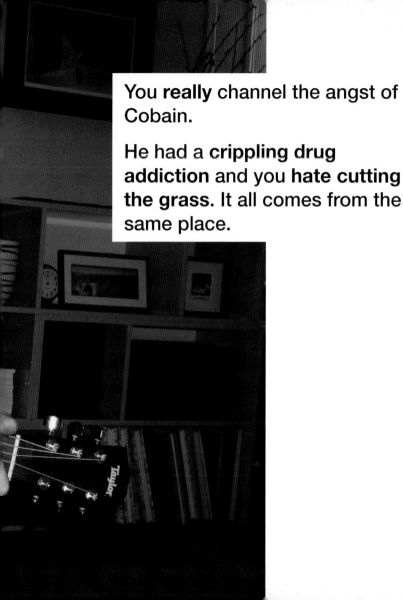

You **really** channel the angst of Cobain.

He had a **crippling drug addiction** and you **hate cutting the grass**. It all comes from the same place.

It's OK. You thought our four-year-old's underwear was mine.

Laundry can be confusing.

Pretty sweet how you **scammed** that pregnant woman out of her seats.

Maybe we can **dine and dash** somewhere after the game.

You're a **great** son, honey.

Any mom would be **proud** to listen to your whining **four to six times per week.**

You're **still** King of Spontaneous Roadtrips, babe.

All you need is your sunglasses, allergy meds, Imodium, and **poof**—you're on the road like Kerouac.

Just because you'd rather let the dog pee in the house than get up and walk him during the night doesn't mean you're lazy. I call it **"principled."**

Awww, I know getting out of bed with the sniffles is hard.

Just like when I shoveled the driveway with double pneumonia.

That hot new intern is **definitely** into you.

I mean, **why else** would she ask you to buy her beer?

Don't worry about leaving your empty beer bottles out overnight.

Our two-year-old needs **something to play with** in the morning.

You were **great** last night honey.

Leaving your socks on is **so kinky!**

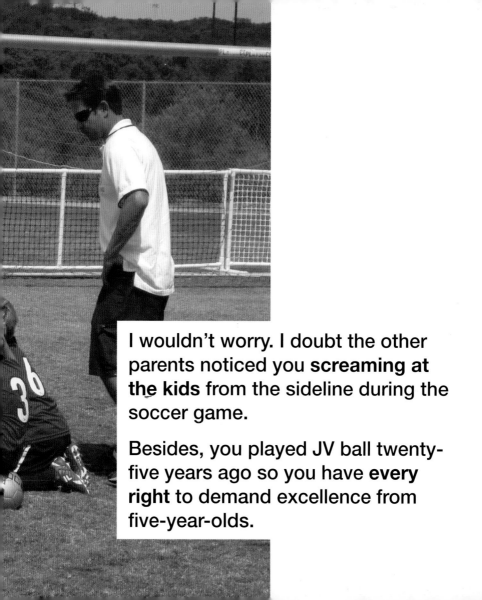

I wouldn't worry. I doubt the other parents noticed you **screaming at the kids** from the sideline during the soccer game.

Besides, you played JV ball twenty-five years ago so you have **every right** to demand excellence from five-year-olds.

How were you supposed
to remember that **I hate
anchovies?**

I only threw up **that one
time,** and that was **almost** a
year ago.

Your band is **totally** going to make it.
How do I know?

Because you just **blew the freaking doors off** the Veterans' Hall with that rendition of "Stairway to Heaven."

You've **sure got a system** with those dishes.

But **how many more days** do you think the pots and pans need "to soak"?

Of course I don't mind if you sign up again for the office's coed softball team.

Throwing back shots at the Grumpy Pelican with twenty-two-year-old assistants is just **another step toward the corner office.**

I **love** our dinner conversations.

And you've become **quite the accomplished nose whistler,** by the way.

Thank you for pushing me to stay current with **my** style.

Lord knows **yours is timeless.**

I like going to the **same old place** for dinner every time.

Like you always say, when you find a "killer spinach dip," **why go anywhere else?**

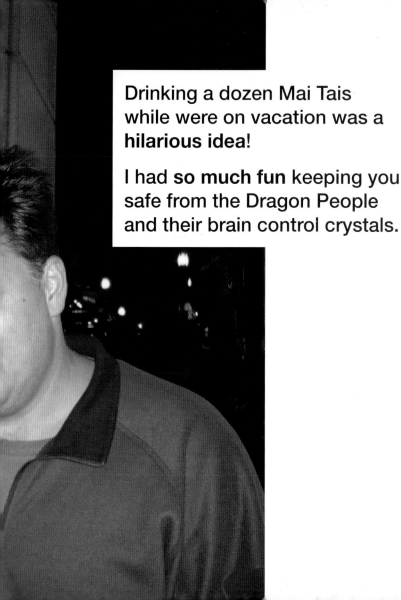

Drinking a dozen Mai Tais while were on vacation was a **hilarious idea!**

I had **so much fun** keeping you safe from the Dragon People and their brain control crystals.

Acknowledgments

One man alone cannot assemble such an astonishing work of literary genius. I'd like to thank my editor, Brendan O'Neill, for keeping the book and me focused; Brad "Scope" Copeland for supplying so many great shots for so little in return; and Brad DeMarea, Jared ElMofty, Andy Kohman, and Randy Myers for graciously agreeing to be non-flattering subjects, as well as everyone else who sent in such humiliating photos—your lack of pride astounds me.

About the Author

Dan Consiglio writes for a living and a hobby. By day, he creates commercials, print ads, websites, and more for brands large and small. His first book, *The New Dad from A to Z* (Andrews McMeel Publishing, 2010), provides freaked-out, first-time dads with some simple, practical advice in a short attention–span format. Dan also co-wrote and directed a feature-length film, *alleyball*, which won nice acclaim on the festival circuit and played in several cities across the United States. Not surprisingly, the film follows five guys in Chicago who prefer playing Wiffle ball instead of dealing with reality. Dan lives in Chicago with his patient wife and three children.

Photo Credits

Page 6 by Dan Consiglio
Page 8 by Morgan Bradley
Page 11 by Michelle Roy Kelly
Page 12 by Dan Consiglio
Page 14 by Brad DeMarea
Page 16 by Will Meyers
Page 18 by Dan Consiglio
Page 20 © iStockphoto/restyler
Page 21 © 123RF and
  iStockphoto/typoonski
Page 22 by Dan Consiglio
Page 24 by Shawn Baldwin
Page 26 © iStockphoto/framers
Page 27 by James Schwartz
Page 28 by Lucy Consiglio
Page 31 by Dan Consiglio
Page 33 by Deb Drumm
Page 34 by Brad Copeland
Page 36 © 123RF
Page 38 by Dan Consiglio
Page 40 by Will Meyers
Page 42 by Brad Demarea
Page 44 by James Schwartz
Page 47 by Kristin Kohman
Page 48 by Lauren Consiglio
Page 49 © iStockphoto/
  Pashalgnatov

Page 50 by Andrew Gall
Page 52 by Andrew Gall
Page 54 by Lauren Consiglio
Page 56 by John Reid
Page 58 by Dan Consiglio
Page 59 © iStockphoto/Imo
Page 60 by Phil Flickinger
Page 63 by Brad Copeland
Page 64 © iStockphoto/
  donald_gruener
Page 66 by Dan Consiglio
Page 68 by Dan Consiglio
Page 69 © iStockphoto/kreinick
Page 71 by Ron Villacarillo
Page 72 by Brad Copeland
Page 75 by Billy Moran
Page 76 by Andrew Gall
Page 78 by Gerald Mortensen
Page 80 by Kellynn Meeks
Page 83 by Dan Consiglio
Page 84 by David Estoye
Page 86 by Jack McLaughlin
Page 87 © iStockphoto/
  rKIRKimagery
Page 88 by Dan Consiglio
Page 90 by Brad Copeland
Page 93 by Deb Drumm